Globalization and International Trade

to Accompany

Economics Today
Eighth Edition
and
Updated Eighth Edition

both by

Roger LeRoy Miller
University of Texas
Arlington, Texas

Prepared by

James Mason
San Diego Mesa College
San Diego, California

 HarperCollins*CollegePublishers*

GLOBALIZATION AND INTERNATIONAL TRADE to accompany
Miller, *Economics Today*, Updated Eighth Edition.

Copyright © 1996 HarperCollins*Publishers*

ISBN: 0-06-502548-2

96 97 98 99 00 9 8 7 6 5 4 3

Table of Contents

INTRODUCTION

In the few short years since the Berlin Wall came down, globalization has emerged as a directing force of world events. Communications and transportation advances are major vehicles that make possible globalization trends.

While consumer demand fueled the huge U.S. economic expansion of the last half of the 20th century, world growth prospects depend on international trade to meet the promise of the 21st century. Such changes will require massive shifts in infrastructure and investment worldwide to accommodate orderly and sustainable growth. These changes are already underway; trends are unmistakable.

Orbital satellites have opened global communications not just for the telephone, but virtually all media forms. Information of any kind in digital form can be processed, transmitted, broadcast or otherwise distributed in unimaginable amounts. The Internet is only one example of capabilities supporting globalization and trade activity.

Communications bring closer cultural and civil activities of diverse groups the world over. Many new products or services are introduced on an international basis. We shall be observing common activities of youth worldwide. Indeed, much of the globalization trend has to do with products and activities of young people. Many key products such as footwear and apparel give insights into globalization trends.

We are living in one of the major watersheds of economic history. Immense changes are in work with all the attendant risks and opportunities. Awareness of the significance and structure of economic change is essential. People who hope to participate in and influence this new age must be well versed in economic principles. The future is both challenging and demanding. Prime rewards will go to those who prepare.

Chapter One

DEMAND/DERIVED DEMAND

The purpose of this chapter. . . is to expand on elements of demand and derived demand and to connect them with globalization and unfolding world events.

Important Terms:

appreciation / depreciation
comparative advantage
derived demand
determinants of demand
devaluation
economic cost
economies of scale
free port
GDP

industrially advanced
  countries
maquiladoras
multinational corporation
NAFTA
newly industrialized
  countries
social cost

Economics Today Cross References:

Introduction

American pop culture has rapidly become a prime mover of globalization and trade. Consumer choices among young adults from both **industrially advanced countries** (IACs) and **newly industrialized countries** (NIC's) are a significant part of international trade. Demand and related **derived de-**

mands among young consumers reflect much of the rapid change globalization is bringing to patterns of world trade.

Demand is not just wanting something. For demand to be effective, people have to *want* to purchase something plus have the income to pay for it *and* the willingness to spend the income. A supply of any good demanded in trade must be made from production input factors. The demand for these factors is *derived* from the demand for the final product. The demand for hip-hop bands is *derived* from the final demand for hip-hop CDs and live concerts.

Critical-Thinking Question:

1. For what reasons would a rational musical group organize themselves into a hip-hop band?

Tastes and Preferences

One of the most powerful **determinants of demand** is people's tastes and preferences. Whether rational or not, people's preferential choices can drive whole markets. In a world divided by trade wars, tribalism, and other hostilities, young people have become an integrating force. Whether in L.A., Tokyo, or Rio, new consumers exhibit a surprisingly common set of tastes and preferences for everything from clothing (Levis/ Reeboks) to soft drinks (Classic Coke/ Pepsi Max) to electronics (Macintosh/ Motorola Beepers).

Fueling this effective demand is income earned by part-time employment. This has given young consumers an independence from parental dominance. In the U.S. alone, this group spends slightly more than $60 billion of their own earnings yearly. They buy a quarter of all movie tickets and videos; nearly tripled purchases of jeans from 1990-95, topping out sales at $2.1 billion. They spend twice that on sneakers. Definitely big business!

These tastes and preferences show up on MTV and other TV channels that cater to popular tastes worldwide. The images shown have become the consumer choices for great numbers of young people worldwide who see and are moved to imitate. When a new pop product is introduced in the U.S., it will instantly follow on in up to 137 other countries.

Many products are international to start with. Reebok shoes, made in several foreign countries by a **multinational corporation**, sell equally well in the U.S., Brazil, Mexico, or Europe. Markets boggle the mind—for 10 to 19 year olds in key Latin American countries an estimated 59 million potential buyers reside compared to 36 million in the U.S.

In the same age group (10–19), the NIC's of Asia boast a market population of 42 million—about 18 percent of the population compared to 14 percent for the U.S. Europe is not as influenced by U.S. pop culture, but has 50 million young consumers who buy much less than the U.S. market. Nonetheless, these are powerful and critical markets for companies that make and sell the desired products.

Access to global young adult markets is made principally through television and advertising. Increasingly, youth of all nations are accepting of other countries, cultures, and peoples. Acceptance of cultural diversity in music and foods illustrates the more recent popularity of rap, hip-hop, and spicy foods from around the world. Hard-sell ads appear pushing foot wear, exotic foods, and soft drinks. Bonding to international products during the formative years develops brand loyalties as consumers mature. With such huge ongoing markets, **economies of scale** become more than impressive; as production increases, marginal cost per unit of output goes down, increasing marginal unit profits.

Critical-Thinking Questions:

1. Will tastes and preferences affect currency values as the consumer market matures?
2. Will youth employment statistics necessarily affect the allocation of advertising dollars?

Derived Demand

As more young Mexicans want to buy U.S. jeans, pesos must be exchanged for dollars. In this way, the demand for dollars is derived from the demand for U.S. products. With the supply of dollars constant, increased demand by Latino youths for American products will increase (**appreciate**) the value of the dollar against the peso. That is, it will take more pesos to buy a dollar. The peso will **depreciate** against the dollar, meaning that a dollar will buy more pesos than before.

The 1995 devaluation of the peso was an official move by the Mexican government that, among other things, makes Mexican exports more salable abroad. The move serves to depreciate the peso and makes it more expensive for Mexicans to purchase foreign goods.

International trade creates unanticipated effects on many interdependent areas of individual economies. Interactivity among trading nations will create many domestic policy shifts affecting autonomy of annual budgets and monetary policy. These points will be discussed later.

Critical-Thinking Question:

1. When a currency is devalued, is derived demand for the currency increased or decreased? Explain how

demand for the final product is affected in domestic and foreign markets.

EuroDisney

American pop culture does not always gain acceptance worldwide. The $4 billion investment in EuroDisney, a theme park that opened in suburban Paris April, 1992, illustrates French contrariness.

Due to several managerial miscalculations, high operating costs and a currency change, the park lost $900 million for the year 1993. Europeans do not "cotton" to American pop culture as do young Asians and Latinos. Planning estimates of what Europeans would spend on theme items, eating, and extra rides were based on American theme park data. Actual operating data showed that more conservative Europeans bought about one-third of the expected amounts.

Also, the French did not like the park's alcohol-free policy which Disney would not consider negotiable. Coca-Cola is offensive to the mature French palette. The future of EuroDisney was in doubt, but since that time, several changes have been made.

The alcohol-free policy has been reversed, and operating expenses have been brought into line with actual revenues. Financially, a $43 million cash infusion from an Arab investor has healed working capital deficiencies and reassured stockholders and creditors.

Critical-Thinking Questions:

1. Which of the determinants of demand do you think played the biggest role in the slow start experienced by EuroDisney?
2. Considering the market, would changes in exchange rates have an effect on the "bottom line?"

Maquiladoras

On the border of U.S. and Mexico, the *maquiladora* program illustrates **derived demand** for labor and the principle of **comparative advantage**. The programs are more than 25 years old but form much of the structure for major portions of **NAFTA** (North American Free Trade Agreement) and its effects on both U.S. and Mexican economies. NAFTA is a treaty between the three nations of North America that, in its simplest meaning, allows goods and services to be traded across borders with no tariff barriers. This is similar to the way goods travel among and between the United States.

Maquiladoras involve "twin-plant" arrangements with American companies doing technical portions of production. Semi-finished goods are sent to the Mexican plant for labor intensive assembly, finishing, and packaging. In this way, comparative advantages are exercised on both sides of the border.

The programs increased the demand for Mexican labor and resulted in heavy migration from southern Mexico to the northern border states. Because of these changes, about 18 percent of the Mexican population lives in the border states and produces more than 28 percent of the country's **GDP**, which is the sum of final sales of all goods and services produced by the economy in a year. All these changes derived from exercising comparative advantage.

After NAFTA, the shift of labor-intensive work to Mexico will be accelerated, a process that will deplete U.S. unskilled employment opportunities and increase Mexican population shifts to the northern border states. The process will place heavy burdens on the principal cities of the border states for housing, sanitation, police protection, etc. Long term, NAFTA will send development deeper into the border states as **economic** and **social costs** of border development mount.

Critical-Thinking Questions:

1. If currency was issued regionally rather than nationally, would you expect to see higher exchange rates in Mexican border states or in the interior?
2. How would a single currency between the U.S. and Mexico affect the *maquiladora* programs?

"Freeport" Guantanamo

Cuban refugees trying to go to the U.S. are intercepted by the Coast Guard in the Florida Straits, then taken to the U.S. Naval Base at Guantanamo Bay. There they are interned in temporary tent-city camps.

It has been suggested, somewhat tongue-in-cheek, that because of this supply of labor, Guantanamo ought to be turned into a **free port**; a kind of Hong Kong on the Caribbean. Free ports have the advantages of being duty-free for importing or exporting of goods and services. They tend to attract investment funds because of limited government regulation.

Let investors organize that labor source, make it self-sufficient and embarrass the Castro government with high levels of productivity. The venture could well supply entrepreneurs for a new Cuba and serve as an example for democratic capitalism.

The cheap labor markets of the world will be tapped by enterprising investors seeking to exercise comparative advantage. As labor markets get more expensive, they must shift to more efficient and productive production schemes to stay competitive.

Critical-Thinking Question:

1. What factors other than inexpensive labor make Cuba an ideal free port location?

Chapter Two

GOVERNMENT-IMPOSED PRICE CONTROLS

The purpose of this chapter . . . is to examine the effects of price controls imposed upon goods and transactions in the global marketplace.

Important Terms:

appreciation (currency)
balance of payments
balance of trade
barriers to trade
black market
capital
capital gains
ceiling price
depreciation (currency)
derived demand

export / import
GATT
multinational company
normative
price support system
subsidy
surplus / shortage
tariff / duty / quota
yield

Economics Today Cross References:

Introduction

Governments are intimately involved with international trade. Government's hand is constructive in providing a rule of law for international contracts, agency, and torts. Also, it may try to influence the outcome of justice and commerce with **normative** (value judgmental) schemes and adjustments that may work contrary to desired results. In addressing domestic public opinion, governments sometime adopt policies that do not benefit international trade. Also, domestic policy manipulations may run contrary to export development.

Among these more controversial areas is price controls, particularly in the form of **barriers to trade; tariffs** (import taxes), **duties** (administrative charges), and **quotas** (agreed-on limits to imports). Public policies can encourage or deny a flow of trade goods.   These can be calculated policies of expedience or inadvertent results from vague and/or naïve theories.

Critical-Thinking Question:

1. How do barriers to trade benefit domestic suppliers? Is this a short-run or long-run gain?

Mixed Blessings

During the Reagan years (1981-89), interest rates were elevated, strengthening (**appreciating**) the dollar against most world currencies. Many foreigners wanted to buy U.S. Treasury bonds because of the high **yield** (percent interest paid on the investment) and an appreciating dollar. Demand for U.S. securities created a **derived demand** for dollars with which to buy the securities.

With lowered tariff barriers at U.S. ports of entry, it was easy and attractive for Americans to buy foreign-made goods with high-value dollars. With lower priced quality goods available, domestic producers could not pass on cost increases without losing market share. While contemporary policies had benefits, they also had costs: a boon to American consumers also created a growing trade deficit.

Critical-Thinking Questions:

1. If the dollar began depreciating, would foreign investors still want to buy U.S. bonds?
2. Can you describe how increased competition in the foreign sector kept inflation down in the U.S.?

Exodus of U.S. Investment

A U.S. investor could take high-value dollars overseas and buy much more with her financial **capital** than she could get at home. Add to this a 52 percent corporate tax rate and an effective 20 percent **capital gains tax,** (paid on realistic long-term increased value of investments) and it was no wonder U.S. capital left home. Many **multinational companies** flourished in this economic climate.

An American tennis shoe maker could go to Taiwan or Korea and make three to four times the number of shoes abroad with his capital. With low tariffs for importation into the U.S., profitability was relatively high. These incentives sent labor-intensive manufacturing jobs and investment overseas in automobiles, textiles, and eventually consumer electronics manufacturing

Critical-Thinking Question:

1. Why would a foreign investor purchase stocks and bonds in America, but avoid manufacturing here?

Trade Surpluses and Deficits

The lesson in all of this is that exchange rates have a profound effect on international trade. The rates affect the amounts that nations **export** and **import** (balance of trade) and the formation of capital surpluses or deficits (**balance of payments**).

During the 1980's the U.S. balance of trade deficit grew rapidly. One major assault was the growing U.S. deficit with Japan. This heavy and growing outflow of dollar credits put enormous sums in the hands of the Japanese. Japan did not want to reciprocate and buy U.S. consumer goods (they were and are buyers of our capital goods). Since 1968, they could not claim U.S. gold. They did the next thing which was to purchase other U.S. assets. Not only bonds and stocks, but commercial real estate and businesses. When the Emperor's Palace is valued at more than the state of California, you buy Pebble Beach!

With the softening (depreciation) of the dollar in recent years, it has been harder for foreign manufacturers to sell products in the U.S. and to maintain both market share and profitability. A cheaper dollar makes it more expensive for Americans to buy Japanese-made goods. In their determination to hold on to market share, Japanese auto firms have been less profitable since the mid-1980's and have countered by building auto assembly plants in the U.S. to avoid exchange rate problems. This action helps repatriate U.S. payment deficit dollars and reinstates profits for Japanese makers. It also increases U.S. auto employment.

Critical-Thinking Questions:

1. Explain how an appreciation in the value of the yen against the dollar will affect U.S. exports.

2. Would a rational Japanese investor with "excess" dollars choose to hold those dollars rather than to invest in American stocks, bonds and real estate? Explain.

Agricultural Subsidies

For political reasons, governments create support pricing schemes to keep less than efficient farms operating. In so doing, **surpluses** are created in some markets, while prices are raised in others. Some policies make direct payments (**subsidies**) to farmers. In any case, consumers are denied purchase of products at lower world prices. Subsidy payments come in the form of higher market prices or higher taxes to support the public sector scheme.

International trade will put downward pressure on world prices. Increasingly, the tax burden of maintaining agricultural subsidies is coming under political pressure. General Agreement on Tariffs and Trade (**GATT**) conferences and World Trade Organization policies are isolating countries that want to continue farm subsidies

The European Union (EU) has agreed to reform its Common Agricultural Policy, reflecting more the current U.S. system of direct subsidies to farmers (deficiency payments) rather than expensive and inefficient **price support systems**.

But, while EU has agreed, France, a nation with a strong agricultural lobby, withheld support. France wants measures negotiated that would minimize displacement of the *status quo*. French agricultural policy is complex, convoluted, and closely interacting with import/export policies. This will be a contentious issue with the French for many years to come.

Variations in world trade policy create opportunities for illegal market activities. West African nations have had, in recent years, thriving **black markets** in cereal grains. High world demand coupled with lax trade laws have diverted up to one-third (200,000 tons per year) of West African grains into (illegal) re-export market channels. Because of the disruption of distribution, famine can develop in third world countries even in years of record farm output. Wars and other civil strife only add to the inefficiency.

Critical-Thinking Questions:

1. How would a government subsidy of grain affect exports of grain from that country?
2. How might a nation's trading partners react to these subsidy programs?

Black Markets

Normative governmental pricing policies can affect more than farm product distribution. Black markets can develop anywhere suppliers cannot (or will not) produce enough product to satisfy quantity demanded at the given price. Normally, prices are bid upward, rationing out excess buyers in the process.

When **ceiling prices** (below true market prices) are imposed on legal markets, **shortages** develop. Quantity demanded exceeds quantity supplied. The excess quantity demanded swells buying pressure at lower than natural price levels. But official prices cannot be raised. The result is diversion of supplies into black markets where higher prices are bid by people who are willing and able to pay. Many third-world economies function effectively only because of illegal market allocations.

Exploitation of black markets is fairly common in world trade. Examples from the recording industry relate to this theme. Shortages of CDs, audio tapes, and videos are being filled by bootleg operations worldwide. Asian countries are especially involved. Copyright and intellectual property protections are part of all major trade agreements (e.g. GATT) since 1987. Increasingly, foreign courts are recognizing the need to enforce patent and copyright law as many of their own nationals are being hurt by piracy. Stiff fines and prison sentences are being given to foreign national offenders.

Policing is difficult and only artists and inventors with substantial resources can pursue court action. In recent years, several benchmark cases have reinforced international copyright law. The German Federal Supreme Court held that release of CD albums of previously released Rolling Stones hits was illegal. Boxed sets of Elvis Presley recordings were part of illegally proliferated "re-released" CDs ordered destroyed by the European court.

Black markets abound worldwide as much because of laws as in spite of them. Precious stones, electronic devices, computers, and apparel are all traded on illegal markets. One of the biggest and growing black markets is in former Soviet military equipment peddled to third-world countries. Since dissolution of the Soviet state, third-world countries have lost the protective patronage of either the Soviet or U.S. military. They desire to protect their self-interests from aggressive neighboring states.

Critical-Thinking Questions:

1. How does black market activity affect the circular flow model? GDP? Governmental tax collection?
2. How does black market activity contribute to corruption in business and government?

Chapter Three

OPEN-ECONOMY TRANSMISSION MECHANISM

The purpose of this chapter. . . is to examine the effects of international monetary policies on trade and national income.

Important Terms:

central banks
dirty float
European Exchange Rate
 Mechanism
floating exchange rates
G-5, G-7, G-10
hedging
international monetary

market
money markets
privatization
public debt
public sector
recession
yield

Economics Today Cross References:

Chapter 16 Monetary Policy
Chapter 24 Monopoly
Chapter 28 Resource Demand and Supply
Chapter 33 Comparative Advantage and Open
             Economy

Introduction

The international monetary system is an integral part of globalization and trade. Money and credit circulates like blood to keep the world system vital and growing.

While there is no central international bank, cooperation among and between the major **central**

banks (bankers' banks that serve and regulate a nation's commercial banks) of trading nations is necessary for the efficient functioning of international trade. Efforts to achieve and maintain this cooperation can be seen in such associations of nations as the **Group of 5 (G-5), Group of 7 (G-7), or Group of 10 (G-10).**

Domestic policy changes in many major trading nations create waves and turbulence in world monetary markets where nations' currencies are traded. The international system constantly seeks equilibrium and a certain amount of chaos is to be expected.

A major outcome of efforts to achieve equilibrium in monetary markets may lead to a total reorganization of the structure, exchange rates, and interrelationships between money systems and commercial trade. One thing is certain; the future will be anything but dull or boring.

Critical-Thinking Question:

1. Why is equilibrium in the international money market important for trade?

Dirty Float

Since summer of 1971, world currencies have been on **floating exchange rates.** That is, they trade against one another with values rising or falling daily depending on economic and political circumstances.

Floating rates are subject to manipulation by large commercial concerns or, especially, central banks of large trading nations. This intervention distorts short-run values of currencies and is called a **"dirty float."** For instance, if Japan was about to sell a large number of autos to U.S. distributors and the dollar was weakening, some large Japanese bank or consortium of banks might buy dollars for future delivery to sustain the dollar's value temporarily and make the auto transaction profitable. The group could **hedge** any losses in dollar purchases with **short sales** of dollars in a different month. Selling short anticipates a drop in value of a currency. Profit is assured by selling first and buying back later at a lower price.

Many international transactions are similarly hedged. In order for Americans to buy German goods, U.S. dollars must be converted to deutche marks (DM). This will be done somewhere in the system through the **international monetary market**.

A merchant has purchased German goods for future delivery at a value of 1.85 DM/ Dollar. At the same time the merchant can purchase the needed amount of DM for future delivery at a quotation of 1.85/1. When the goods are delivered, the prevailing rate for DM is 1.95/1. The merchant buys DM at 1.95 and sells his futures contract for a .10 profit. Subtracting the profit from 1.95 means that the merchant has bought his DM for the desired 1.85/1.

Of course, DM rates could just as well have appreciated to 1.75/1. In that case would the merchant be better off? Not at all! In this case DM would be purchased at market for 1.75/1, but the futures contract would be losing .10. This loss, added to the market price of DM brings the transaction value to 1.85/1, the targeted amount.

In either case, the merchant is *hedged*; he has forgone risk of loss or gain to assure delivery of the needed DM at a specific time and exchange rate. Hedging is done by many international businesses to avoid unforeseen rate changes experienced in volatile monetary markets.

Critical-Thinking Questions:

1. When central banks purchase another currency, how is the exchange rate between that currency and their own affected?
2. Can individuals hedge in international monetary markets? Would this be practical?

Monetary Policies and Effects

International trade and principle markets are divided in three parts; North America, Western Europe, and Asia. Monetary actions of central banks within these three global hubs are both formative of economic policies and reactive to policy effects.

U.S. Monetary Policy

In the United States, since the early 1980's, Federal Reserve Bank (FRB) policies have focused on reducing inflation. Policies have been effective in keeping U.S. inflation rates low and fairly stable for nearly 15 years.

Some of this policy relied on high interest rates (both relative and real) throughout the 1980's. This policy facilitated increases in public debt by reducing the prices of U.S. Treasury bonds. High **yields** and low prices made such bonds attractive all over the world. More and more of our **public debt** was held by foreign creditors.

During the early 1990s, central bank policy changed to the easing of short term rates in order to stimulate growth. Starting in 1994, fears of resurgent inflation (evidenced by rise in commercial metals and gold prices) caused the Fed to tighten Federal funds rates. These are the funds made available for interbank loans, usually on an overnight basis to preserve liquidity.

Aside from the controversy over rates and perceived inflation, U.S. public debt (sum of treasury bonds, notes, and T-bills) must remain attractive to foreign investors. An exodus of foreign money to other international debt instruments would result in a drop in U.S. Treasury bond prices, and a precipitous rise in domestic interest rates. That would more than likely induce a major **recession** in the U.S. economy, a phenomenon that could spread world wide.

U.S. monetary policy is held hostage to nominal international rates, long term. As foreign money markets raise interest rates, the U.S. must follow in order to maintain its share of bond sales.

European Monetary Policy

A significant recovery for Britain has been laid to low inflation, flexible labor rules, and pro-business government policy. Britain is expected to have the best real growth rate in Western Europe for 1995.

Britain's policies have attracted investment from Japan and Germany. Japan's Nissan has invested $1.43 billion since 1984 and employs close to 5,000 British subjects. BMW paid $1.2 billion for Britain's Rover Group, evidence of the British comeback in autos, component parts, and electronics.

British exit from the **European Exchange Rate Mechanism** in 1992 precipitated a steep devaluation of the pound. As a result, labor rates were cut down to $12.90/hour, one-third less than Western Europe's average. On the continent, high corporate and payroll taxes continue to contribute to high unemployment rates and low economic growth.

Asian Monetary Policy

Japan's long slump has much monetary basis. Low Domestic interest rates sent money out of the country, when 10-year Japanese government bonds earned 3.9 percent and 30-year U.S. Treasuries yielded 6.8 percent. Also, Japan's predicament is due in part to yen overvaluation from heavy trade surpluses. These are some of the actions that will contribute to the recovery of the dollar and the slide of the yen:

- Japanese corporations retain more of dollars earned in profits from U.S. manufacturing plants.
- A rise in U.S. interest rates that will favor the dollar vis-a-vis falling Japanese rates.
- Mutual support of the dollar by U.S. and Japanese central bank policy in an attempt to stabilize anxious securities markets
- Erosion of Japanese trade surplus as Japanese manufacturers increasingly go off-shore to seek lower cost base.

Critical-Thinking Questions:

1. Explain how low labor rates ultimately influence currency value, *ceteris paribus* ?
2. What kinds of fiscal policies might counteract the above chain of events?

Privatization

A big part of globalization is a shift away from dependence on **public sector** economic stimulus from federal, state, and local governments. As part of this change, we see increasing sell-offs of productive assets owned by the public sector—a process called **privatization**.

Squeezed by heavy deficits, governments all over the world are selling off assets to raise revenue. The Soviet dissolution is the most dramatic, but we can see the trend even in Orange County, California. After its huge bond losses, the County entertained bids for such things as John Wayne Airport and other public assets to raise as much as $5 billion.

In Europe, many corporate operations that were public/private mixed enterprises are being spun-off. Optimistically, these sales should give the surviving private entity better access to capital markets and improvements in global competitiveness. Some countries, like France, project a total revenue flow of up to $50 billion over a 5 year period.

Europe generally has the biggest potential sale of assets, estimating 75 percent of the total that will go to foreign buyers. Private investors will be wary, however. Some governments are putting tight restrictions on purchases. Belgium insists on job guarantees for employees. France limits to 20 percent the portion of shares that can be sold to interests outside the European Union. The heaviest offerings run in three major industries: oil, banking, and telecommunications.

Critical-Thinking Questions:

1. What motives would a government have to privatize an industry?
2. How is international trade affected when a large block of nations, such as the European Union, undertakes privatization schemes simultaneously?
3. Can you develop a transmission mechanism involving unemployment, national income, exchange rates, and international trade when privatization occurs within an industry?

Chapter Four

APPLIED MONETARY POLICY

The purpose of this chapter. . . to further explore how monetary policy changes affect international trade and challenge global investment and multinational operations.

Important Terms:

appreciate / depreciate
balance of payments
demand-pull
fixed exchange rates
IMF

inflation / hyperinflation
letter of credit
monetizing
yield

Economics Today Cross References:

Introduction

Financial structure and international trade are closely tied. The one influences the other. The more interdependent nations become in trade, the more vulnerable they are to cracks in financial structure. Interest rates, **balance of payments** and **inflation** become a symptomatic scale for judging global economic health.

Inflation and Hyperinflation

Inflation is a general, sustained rise in price levels. Real causes of inflation are not always easy to identify. It's like seeing only the fever without knowing the micro organism that caused the fever. Examining a few historical inflations will give some insight.

After World War I, Germany was strapped with paying reparations to Britain and France. These were shipments of goods sent in payment for damages done in the War. Coupled with Germany's public debt from preparation and conduct of the War (dating from 1910), the post-war reparations piled up more and more public and private debt.

The German government financed all this debt by **monetizing** it through the Reichbank. Debt is monetized when the central bank buys the credits (debt) and issues Reichmarks for it.

As a result, the German public had increasing amounts of money to buy an inadequate supply of goods. Over the years, a classic **"demand-pull"** inflation (lots of money chasing too few goods) expanded into **hyperinflation**. In 1923 there was a 23 million-to-one expansion in Reichmarks. Speculation replaced production and social and political order broke down. In desperation, the Weimar government repudiated the old currency and issued new Marks, which stabilized the economy. In this case, Germany's hyperinflation did not persist.

In contrast, Brazil in the 1980's experienced a long, steady bout with high inflation rates as part of an historical pattern of inflation. Brazil's inflation has never responded well to anti-inflation measures. It was volatile, rising then falling, then bursting forth again explosively. It has been theorized that the Brazilian economy, by its organization and structure, is inherently inflationary. This persistence to inflation has defied attempts to stabilize it.

Another South American economy, Argentina, exhibits similar persistent inflationary characteristics. Much of Argentina's current problems go back to the Peronist era. Jobs were created by concerted expansion of secondary manufacturing industries with no development of basic industries to supply such things as steel and energy.

As a result, Argentina had to import huge quantities if primary materials. Depending on exports of beef and grain to pay for primary imports failed and generated balance of payments deficits. A long history of international borrowing and defaults has followed.

One may be prompted to assume that all these problems with inflation indicate a particular flawed Latin American bias. For the record, Chile has emerged as a viable, growing economy after a turbulent bout with hyperinflation in the 1970's. Chile has come through several decades of volatile political and social change, surviving a military dictatorship to establish a strong market-centered economy. By maintaining balance between money supply growth and anticipated real economic expansion, Chile has emerged as South America's most stable economy.

Critical-Thinking Questions:

1. Why would a nation importing most of its raw materials be susceptible to inflationary pressures?
2. What role does money supply growth play in inflation? In exchange rates?

Exporting Inflation

Until 1971, foreign exchange rates were fixed (pegged) by agreement and maintained through the **International Monetary Fund (IMF).** Members of the fund subscribed to support other member currencies at these fixed rates. Supporting a currency means that the central banks of member nations will always convert foreign currencies at the pegged rate.

In effect, this implies that a wine merchant in the U.S. can send a dollar denominated **letter of credit** to a French wine exporter along with his order. The French exporter will accept the letter because his bank will issue his account a credit for Francs at 5-to-the-dollar. The French commercial bank will do this because the central bank of France will issue a franc credit to the commercial bank. The central bank keeps the dollar credits as a foreign exchange account.

Under the original Bretton Woods agreement, if these dollars were not used to buy U.S. goods or to purchase other foreign goods, they could be sent to the Federal Reserve bank and redeemed in American gold at $35/oz. But after the 1968 dollar crisis, the U.S. gold window was closed and foreign banks had to hold excess dollar credits, effectively monetizing these dollar surpluses into the accepting nation's money supply.

As the American economy inflated, French wines became a bargain in dollar terms compared to inflated U.S. domestic prices. Americans drank more French wine and sent more dollars to France to pay for it. Those dollars served to expand and inflate the French money supply. Soon the burden became too great for central banks to carry, and during summer, 1971, the dollar was floated against all world currencies ending the system of pegged rates. Central banks no longer support member currencies. Anyone who wants French wine must convert their currency to francs in monetary markets at whatever the exchange rate is at that time.

Critical-Thinking Questions:

1. Under fixed exchange rates, how does an accumulation of credits affect a nation's money supply?
2. If international trade represents a large share of nation "A's" income and a small share of nation "B's" income, which nation's balance of payments is more affected by inflation under fixed exchange rates? Under floating exchange rates?

Interest Rates

Interest rate increases have characterized international finance in the mid 1990s. Trade and commerce use huge amounts of available financing. As trade and economic activities pick up, the demand for money and credit increases, too. With any given supply of credit, increased demand will bid up interest rates. Because rates vary inversely to bond prices, any rise in interest rates will cause a corresponding decline in bond (and other securities) prices.

Bonds are a major world source for financing debt. Globalization has created a more universal market for bond funding. In the long run, higher interest rates will siphon-off funding from lower interest markets. All debtors (including governments) must remain competitive and attractive to bond buyers by meeting equilibrium interest rate levels when funding new or refinanced bond issues.

Many people and institutions hold bonds as a source of steady, predictable income; a "safe" place to put money capital. However, there is a speculative element even to the highest grade of bonds. Interest rate changes can have profound effects on this kind of investment. Because bond market prices vary inversely to interest rates, when rates climb, market prices of existing bonds drop. People who hold very short-term obligations are least concerned; if market prices drop, they can wait the few weeks until obligations mature then redeem at full face value.

But, people who are in long-term bonds and who need money must sell before redemption dates. Timing is crucial. Bonds bought at low interest rates will **depreciate** (lose value) as interest rates climb. On the other end of the bond cycle, interest rates are falling and bond prices will be **appreciating**.

As interest rates peak mid-cycle (timing again), purchase of bonds is at reduced (discounted) prices and **yield** is high, creating a good buying opportunity. As interest rates decline, the investor sustains that high rate of return, while the bond price is appreciating. If the bonds are high grade, the capital is relatively safe. With this strategy, the investor gets all three things people invest for: safety of capital, favorable rate of return, and appreciation of capital.

Critical-Thinking Questions:

1. Explain how demand for money function is influenced by bond yields. How does this affect international investment trends?
2. When a nation experiencing inflation has corresponding high interest rates, would its bond market attract international investors?
3. Would bonds be a popular investment, considering the safety of capital aspect, for investors dealing with hyperinflation?

Bond Markets

At times, rising interest rates have created problems in long-term bond markets. Holders of this type of bonds, purchased at relatively low interest rates, are unhappy because they are not participating in the rising rates of return. Also, the market value of the bond holdings is eroding; if bonds had to be sold, there would be a lose of capital. This situation gets more anxious when there are big bond portfolio losses like those in Orange County, California in 1994 and 1995.

Orange County bet on stable or declining interest rates and a slowly rising inflation. To increase portfolio earnings, a portion of the county's bonds were pledged against loans for purchases of additional bonds. This is a "leveraged" position. As interest rates went up, the collateral value of the pledged bonds went down.

The county got a "call" for additional cash to maintain the collateral value of loans. When the cash was not forthcoming, creditors closed out the account position, converting "paper" loses into real loses; about $2 billion worth.

As a general rule, short-term obligations (90 days or less) are held when rates are rising and where there is a good chance redemption for cash will be needed. Otherwise, long-term maturities are held when interest rates are declining, so as to receive above-market rates of return and to participate in market price appreciation. Stable price levels in the economy and lack of inflationary influences also favor holding long-term bonds.

Critical-Thinking Questions:

1. Explain why during rising interest rates bond purchases are regarded as a "graveyard for capital?"
2. What alternatives to bond investments can you think of for the international community to benefit from rising interest rates?

Chapter Five

GLOBAL CAPITAL MARKETS

The purpose of this chapter. . . is to consider the factors creating and influencing capital flows between nations, and to examine trends in policies that impact the balance of trade and corresponding balance of payments.

Important Terms:

appreciated
balance of payments
balance of trade
Bretton Woods agreement
central bank interventions
comparative advantage
depreciation
EU
fixed exchange rate
floating exchange rates

floating rates
fluctuation margins
G-7
J curves
NAFTA
newly industrialized
    countries (NIC)
par values
pegged rates
transmission time

Economics Today Cross References:

Chapter 21   Financial Environment
Chapter 34   Exchange Rates / Balance of Payments

Introduction

With the surge in globalization, money capital flows must respond to an increasingly wide market. The focus for the major flows is still Western Europe **(EU)**, United States **(NAFTA)**, and Japan. In the future, emerging industrial areas of Asia, Latin America, and Eastern Europe will grow in importance and influence regarding capital flow.

Increasing privatization trends and participation in trading blocks have left many **newly industrialized countries (NIC's)** competing on open markets. India, Korea, Argentina, and Turkey have recently become channels of capital flows.

It is not possible to structure so complicated a system here, but we can examine some basic capital flow functions and their relevance to future world development.

Critical-Thinking Question:

1. Why does a market-based economy attract more capital than a command economy?

To Float or Not To Float

The current system of **floating exchange rates,** started in 1971, has some notable problems. Floating rates do not provide a reliable or predictable time for **balance of payments** (capital flow) adjustments between nations experiencing balance of trade deficits or surpluses. Without timely and efficient adjustments of payments accounts, flows of capital are slowed. This creates apparent shortages of capital and increases nominal interest rates.

The measurement of adjustments flow efficiency is done on a graph that compares net export data movement over time. A country that runs a **balance of trade** deficit would register negative net exports. The following realities would be experienced:

- A **depreciation** of its currency in international markets.
- A deepening of its trade deficit, short run.
- A gradual improvement in trade advantage with eventual balance in trade.

The plot of data on a graph produces a characteristic "J" pattern and they are called **J-curves** for that reason. When adjustment processes are well defined and running efficiently, the J curve is of relatively short duration. This indicates that the international system of payments is working well and that capital flows are returning as needed.

When the J curve is flattened, movement is sluggish and time-response increments grow longer. Indications are that the monetary system is inefficient and that capital repatriations are slow. In recent years J curves have become much flatter, giving signs of aging and unresponsiveness in our current international monetary system.

One explanation for this growing inefficiency of capital flow is increased **central bank interventions** to influence currency exchange rates (i.e., a "dirty float"). All of these indicators would seem to call for a new international monetary system. This was done in 1946 with the **Bretton Woods Agreement** that established the post-WW II **fixed exchange rate** system. It was done again by default in 1971 with the present system of **floating rates.** There are a number of alternatives for reform.

Critical-Thinking Questions:

1. Compared to domestic capital markets, what factors in international capital markets account for a "lag" in capital flows?
2. Do you think J-curves are flatter within the EU or between EU and North America?

European Monetary System (EMS)

While worldwide exchange rates "float", within the European Union, a system of **pegged rates** is used to regulate payments flow. Called the **European Monetary System (EMS)**, EU authorities have had difficulty holding to the rigid **par values** for member currencies. In the last couple of years, the EMS has expanded **fluctuation margins** to 15 percent above and below par in an attempt to avoid recurring currency crises and to help reduce interest rate levels. Other major elements of the system were retained:

• Central setting of interest rates.
• Obligation of member nations to follow stability-oriented policies.
• Maintenance of the central bank intervention mechanism.

The net effect of this change was more inefficiency in payment adjustments leading to a collapse in the system in 1994. The question remains whether it is better to float or not to float. Should there be floating exchange rates or pegged rates?

The need for a new or greatly overhauled global monetary system would seem apparent. Current inefficiencies are raising interest rates, interrupting capital flows, and stifling economic growth.

Critical-Thinking Questions:

1. As more nations create or join trading blocks, will exchange rate fluctuations likely increase or decrease?
2. Using the circular flow model, explain how international capital flows can be both a leakage and an injection for any given economy.

Foreign Investment

The classic trade balance case is the ongoing U.S. / Japanese trade deficit. As the yen has **appreciated,** a number of relationships change that offset capital (payments) flow. An appreciating yen and depreciating dollar makes selling Japanese goods to the U.S. relatively more expensive; the price of goods to Americans will rise. Unless Japan cuts profit to maintain market share, higher prices for Japanese goods will benefit U.S. makers whose goods will be more favorably priced, all other things being the same. With these realities, a set of change factors comes into play that tend to level the competitive field and restore payments flows over time:

- Japanese companies (e.g. autos) build assembly plants in the U.S. to make cars for sale here.
- American exports to Japan become cheaper for Japanese buyers, creating profit potential for resellers in Japanese markets.
- Japanese firms mobilize cost-cutting techniques to keep pace with the yen/dollar exchange rate.
- The over-valued yen makes purchase of overseas raw material cheaper for Japanese producers.
- Japanese investment in other world countries turns Asia into an "industrial suburb".

Optimists tend to see currency shifts as inevitable and short term. The dynamics of global markets will keep international capital moving to where it is needed by the most efficient producers. Intervention is still a problem. Through cooperative agreement in the **G-7,** it is thought that most problems can be resolved. We may have to wait for the next major monetary crisis for a final judgment on floating exchange rates.

Critical-Thinking Question:

1. "Leveling the playing field' is a phrase heard often in the U.S./Japan trade relationship: to what extent do factors other than monetary policy come into play?

Future Possibilities

Any number of influences are at work that will impinge on the future course of payments and capital flows. There are the open market supporters that feel market influences will eventually do a better job of system change than all the planners can do.

Some of these "natural forces" include GATT and world trade policy. On the positive side, GATT will reduce many government subsidies that directly or indirectly reduce capital flow and discourage trade. Agricultural subsidies, discussed earlier in this work, are just one example.

International cooperatives within and between trading blocks can serve to bridge trade restrictions. Aerospace companies and other high-tech ventures are good examples. Through this means, **advantages of trade** can be exercised that would have been impossible during the Cold War era (1950-1989). There are still many legitimate concerns over technology transfers and equitable sharing of cost and accomplishments. National security does not become a dead issue with "hands-across-the-table" trade policies.

International trends are at work to reduce restrictions on international banking. The U.S. has some of the most restrictive rules on banking activity that has discouraged foreign banks from opening commercial operations in this country. Trends toward interstate banking, soon to be a reality, will help realign the American banking industry to international capacity

Another dynamic change is happening with the Internet. Information networking serves to decrease **transmission time** and increase quality and quantity of pricing and market information. This trend increases market competition and pressures business to increase operating efficiency.

All of these elements and more will serve to change the face of international trade. All of these activities are part of the globalization process that is rapidly reshaping our world.

Critical-Thinking Questions:

1. Explain how government subsidies to domestic industries impede capital flow.
2. How is comparative advantage achieved when 2 or more countries manufacturers work together to produce a product?
3. What aspects of banking regulations might discourage international investors from opening commercial accounts?

Chapter Six

COMPARATIVE ADVANTAGE

The purpose of this chapter . . . to examine how comparative advantage impacts and determines trade, and how cooperative efforts can impact comparative advantage.

Important Terms:

comparative advantage
consortium
economies of scale
infrastructure
intellectual property

royalty
specialization
subsidies
WTO

Economics Today Cross References:

Chapter 18 Economic Growth
Chapter 33 Comparative Advantage / Open Economy

Introduction

Comparative advantage is the capacity to produce at the lowest cost compared to other alternative means. One of the main features of globalization is the search for positions of comparative advantage in international manufacturing and distribution.

Becoming a low-cost producer is a key element in surviving and/or gaining preeminence in the world of international trade. Much of the future world economy will be shaped by ongoing interactions driven by the search for comparative advantage.

Critical-Thinking Question:

1. What cost advantages does globalization offer producers?

International Cooperatives

Even before NAFTA, limited trade agreements between the U.S. and Canada saw manufacturing in
Canada moving south due to lower labor costs in the
U.S. While situations like this seemed bad for Canada, Canadian exports to the U.S. increased, balanc-
ing trade and payments flows to both sides of the
border.

Faced with the prospect of building costly new
production facilities for gun propellants in the U.S.,
DuPont elected to contract with an underemployed
powder factory in Canada, only 50 miles away from its
up-state New York marketing and distribution facil-
ity. **Economies of scale** in the Canadian plant made
unfeasible the building of new capacity in the U.S.

Alternatives to Production

Increasingly, international cooperation is opening alternatives to production and distribution that would
not exist or would be too costly to maintain in a single
country. Many multinational companies were con-
ceived in and continue to thrive on international cooperation. Auto companies have lowered costs and
penetrated new markets using specialization and
comparative advantage techniques.

Ford Motor Company expanded globalization
opportunities with their Taurus Project. The $3 bil-
lion program utilized full-scale services of both U.S.
and Ford Europe. The project fostered close cooperation between international divisions that changed de-

sign and engineering procedures. This and related organizational changes molded the modernization of the company. While the auto industry has been multinational for decades, Ford has achieved a much higher degree of integration of its international divisions in the past 20 years than most other firms; it has been a model of change and adaptation.

Industries like automobiles have been prime movers in the development of international trade. Approximately 60 percent of U.S. international trade movements are intra-industrial. For instance, Ford's Escort sedan is one of the top selling cars worldwide. Engines and transmissions are made in specialized and integrated plants in Spain and shipped all over the world for assembly. Components are made in numerous countries and shipped to where cars are assembled. There are really no "American made" cars any more. Major parts and assemblies are made where ever comparative advantage dictates. Virtually every auto made today contains at least a significant portion of components that are not made in the country of origin.

ISO 9000

Airbus in Europe assembles commercial aircraft whose components are made in several countries in Europe and around the world. ISO 9000, an international quality-assurance document, sets standards for designated manufacturing processes. With these standards, parts or assemblies can be manufactured by many different companies in many different places, but all parts will be interchangeable and satisfy a single specification. This ISO directive has already revolutionized component purchasing.

The search for comparative advantage will find and utilize many labor markets that are not part of first and second world economies. Many of the NIC's (Newly Industrialized Countries) have emerged as suppliers of manufactured components for the world's major producers of aircraft, autos, or electronics.

Critical-Thinking Questions:

1. Why does production seek out lower-cost labor markets?
2. As automation in production increases and the use of robotics replaces labor utilization, what changes in production do you anticipate?

Joint Research

Much technology transfer is afforded to emerging countries through component manufacturing. As the **infrastructures** (transportation, communication, banks, schools) of Taiwan, Singapore, and Malaysia develop, there will be opportunities to participate in research for parts and sub-systems for new, complicated technical projects. Many of these opportunities will come through the NIC's relationships with more senior economies such as Japan or European Union.

A new supersonic transport aircraft (SST), ideally suited for inter-continental travel, is too costly and risky for a single country or company to develop. By breaking down research and development tasks, nations that will be customers for the new aircraft will also participate in its production. Much of the earnings from R&D provides capital flows that help pay for the purchase of the new aircraft.

Technical advances of the past 20 years have solved many of the vexing problems posed by commercial supersonic flight, problems that shelved the U.S. SST project in 1971. Supersonic *Concordes* have been flown for 20 years by the British and French (12 of the original 16 are still flying). The Russians operated their Tupolev TU-144 until it was grounded in 1984. Projected demand for SST's indicates a possibility for 1,000 aircraft through 2015, mostly on the Pacific Rim routes.

A projected design would carry up to 350 passengers with acceptable seat-mile costs. Fares would cost a 15 percent premium. Lead time for such a project is 10 years from go-ahead to the first operational aircraft. Research would involve all major systems of the aircraft including power plants, composite materials and airframe, and avionics. Feasibility studies are underway with a **consortium** of cooperating companies including Aerospatiale (France), British Aerospace, Deutsche Airbus, Boeing and McDonnell Douglas. Alenia (Italy), Japan Aircraft Industries, and Russia's Tupolev have joined the project most recently. Transportation development is one of the major areas of economic expansion (along with communications) that will build and facilitate international trade.

Critical-Thinking Questions:

1. Why is international cooperation, such as joint research, important for future sales when undertaking a high-cost project?
2. How is comparative advantage determined when several companies representing different countries form a production consortium?

GATT

The ratifying of **GATT** treaties marks a commitment into globalization not previously attempted. The process and the agreements are highly controversial, aside from just reducing trade barriers.

World Trade Organization

While the original structure dates from the 1960's, the latest GATT structure directly limits how much a sovereign government can interfere with "natural" market mechanisms. The **World Trade Organization (WTO),** a governing body established through the GATT, will have powers to limit actions by member states. In addition, the WTO may be able to override established laws of sovereign governments that are in conflict with GATT policy. Many conflicts of interest will come out of the process of globalization and whole new areas of international law are expected to develop.

Not the least of these conflicts will involve "protection of a way of life" arguments that have already surfaced regarding U.S., Canadian, and French farming communities. These countries **subsidize** farming sectors by giving payments to sustain inefficient farms, a policy that is not permitted by the GATT accord. There is already controversy over how these changes will be implemented.

Intellectual Properties

Much of U.S. support for GATT centered on increased enforcement by foreign governments for **intellectual property rights.** Piracy of U.S. Patents and copyrighted materials is common, especially in Asia. The GATT requires all member governments to enforce these rights according to common standards. For the first time, software companies, publishers and trademarked goods makers will be able to extend enforcement of protected intellectual properties into the international arena.

How effective this enforcement will be only time will tell. In Europe, some significant cases have been reported out favorably in major court actions. In Asia, the story is not so good. Many Asian governments lack the capacity to enforce effectively. Others are still biased in favor of domestic violators.

A Korean entertainer, after coming home from a tour in the U.S. copyrighted the name "James Dean" in Korea and used it on a chain of stores and trade marks that sell clothing and personal entertainment items. Dean's family, who own the rights to the use of the name sued for payment of **royalties**. The Korean court found that Dean was not famous in Korea and denied the motion, allowing only minor royalties on garment items sold outside Korea.

The world is a vastly different place from what it was even a half-generation ago. Prospects are for even more change in the immediate future. At the base of international expansion will be principles of comparative advantage shaping and directing motivation, behavior, and economic activity.

Critical-Thinking Questions:

1. Why have intellectual property rights become more significant in recent years?
2. If participation in trade based on GATT directives hinges upon enforcement of intellectual property rights, would you expect to see any realignment of trade? How will the flow of income be affected?

Chapter Seven

INVESTMENT AND GROWTH

The purpose of this chapter... to look at the infrastructure required for economic growth and determine the elements necessary for international investment.

Important Terms:

account surpluses
capital goods
Malthusian theory
market-oriented

normative v. positive
optimal population
private property rights
privatization

Economics Today Cross References:

Introduction

Globalization and unity of markets holds great promise for advancement of world affairs. The potential for worldwide investment and growth stagger the imagination. But there are many demands, much sacrifice and change necessary in order to attain the possibilities. Several prerequisites for globalization are in place. Much background structure must still be built and some requirements may never be realized.

The attainment of a viable, functioning postindustrial global community with sustainable economic growth is possible, but probably not in its idealistic form. It is not a given that a global economy will emerge and prosper. Its final form most likely will differ considerably from descriptions that are part of the current hype.

Critical-Thinking Question:

1. With all the technology, treaties, and good wishes for globalization, what could possibly happen to make it fail?

Globalization in Perspective

Most people who talk about globalization do not really know what it is and is not. In concrete terms, globalization involves primarily trade in goods and, to a much smaller extent, trade in services. It includes the international movement of labor and international flows of capital and information. Shifts to non-traded services run counter to globalization trends. Technologies in time will make services like professional skills, transportation, banking, and construction more tradable.

In terms of worldwide economic integration, the world today is about where it was in the late 19th century. But, today, things happen faster and in greater volume. There have been global economies before. Britain, during the Victorian period and up to World War I, averaged payment **account surpluses** of about 4 percent of GDP for forty years before 1914. Roughly, this is what Japan did in the peak of the 1980's. Columbus started one of the biggest and longest running globalizations in history.

In the U.S., the economy maintains relative imports of about 11 percent of GDP, up from 8 percent estimated for the 1880's over a century ago. Labor mobility was very high then and is reduced today by immigration laws. As a portion of world output, the value of worldwide trade in goods and services is only slightly larger today than it was before 1914.

What is different today, and promises to change in the future, is the speed of communication and transportation. These two technologies are the basis for current trends. They distinguish our contemporary globalization from all others. The major positive factor is the shear volume, quality, and reliability of exchange. Financial systems depend on rapid and voluminous communications. Finance ultimately controls the flow of trade and movements of short term capital.

A few final insights will serve to complete the perspective:

- Global economies have come and gone.
- There is no guarantee of globalization's success.
- Less than one-tenth of interested concerns get involved.
- Instant information is the key difference in today's global trend. Communication greases the wheels of commerce.
- Whatever shape globalization takes, the form will grow out of interaction rather than from planned **normative** notions.

Critical-Thinking Questions:

1. With networking services such as Internet, Prodigy, and America On-line, do individuals have the same globalization opportunities as corporations?
2. Why does the finance industry rely more on the speed of information and communication than other industries?

Environmental Issues

Much concern is expressed over the capacity of the earth and its environment to support an expanding global economy. These concerns generally are projected in terms of today's circumstances and do not consider how the world will change.

To succeed, the globalization movement will have to bring on-line and utilize appropriate technologies to meet several environmental concerns. One of these is how to feed a world with 8, 10, or 12 billion population. These same concerns were popular in the 1960's and now again 30 years later. These attitudes reflect earlier **Malthusian** observations (early 1800's) regarding unfavorable predictions about population growth and food production. Malthus believed population would progress geometrically while food supply would grow arithmetically. He predicted that without population control, economic failure would occur by 1850.

Agricultural Productivity

One of the greatest success stories in world history has been the increase in output and efficiency of farm production. Worldwide there are grain supply increases relative to demand as indicated by steadily declining grain prices over the past 20 years, even through periods of high inflation. All this was at a time of high population increases. Where famine has been a factor, poor distribution has been the cause, not waning farm production. In Rwanda, starvation came as a result of civil war. The country was about to harvest bountiful crops as the slaughter began. Many crops rotted in the fields.

Grain surpluses have caused 46 million acres in the U.S. and 11 million acres in EU to be allocated out of production to trim surpluses. If the time comes when more land is needed for cultivation, South America has 200 million acres of savanna that has never seen the plow. This and more is available for future needs, demand and free trade permitting.

In order to check erosion of farm lands, reduce fertilizer and pesticide run-off, and increase plant quality, technologies have the capabilities to do the following things:

- Construct no-till planters that avoid conventional general plowing that exposes the soil to wind and water erosion.
- Global Positioning Systems with COMSAT information can determine seed and fertilizer spread rates to increase yields and cut waste.
- DNA research will produce more productive and disease resistant plants to satisfy growing conditions worldwide.

Population Growth

World population is quite young. The number of young women of child-bearing age is trended upward. Changes in attitudes in emerging countries toward size of families and contraception contribute to achieving **optimal population** growth. Optimal population coincides with the high point of the average output curve in the society, at the point where average and marginal output are equal. At this point, the society feeds the most people to the best possible standards.

After World War II, Indonesia overhauled its agricultural industry and rapidly increased rice production. Not only did this stabilize the economy, but produced enough for export. With this export surplus, Indonesia was able to import **capital goods** and technological services to develop its energy industry.

Things were going so well, people had lots of children; population boomed along with the economy.

Today rising population is rapidly eating all the rice output, reducing the export potential. This is a good example of emerging countries that must control population growth if they are to benefit long term from industrial growth. It also illustrates that agricultural self-sufficiency is a major primary goal for most countries that expect to emerge from poverty.

Industrial Pollution

A big concern of NAFTA opponents was increased pollution in Mexico's northern border states as production activity increases. This surely will happen. Mexico currently does not have the resources to expand production investment and meet pollution standards. These facts have been true for most every emerging economy, including the U.S. 70 to 80 years ago.

As economies mature and produce increasing surpluses, the ability to clean up pollution grows. In this time frame, societies will control or eliminate pollution sources if the commitment is there. The World Trade Organization will also apply pressures on emerging countries to clean up their industrial scene. We see many countries with seriously stressed environments as a result of surging industry. The former Soviet Union and mainland China are stellar examples.

Critical-Thinking Questions:

1. We are familiar with the concerns of overpopulation; can you envision the economic imbalances that would occur in a situation of underpopulation?
2. What factors would shift the optimal population point backward? (Hint: see marginal cost/benefit curves—page 741 in *Economics Today*, 8th Edition)

Socio-Political Aspects of Privatization

A major obstacle to globalization is the conversion of former socialist states to **market oriented** economies. After three generations of command control, these former socialist countries will not quickly or efficiently convert to market operation. One process involves **privatization**, selling off of publicly owned properties to private bidders.

Establishment of **private property rights** takes time. Institutions such as courts and private businesses do not spring up over night. In spite of able and well meaning professional consultants, each former socialist country will have to mold and shape its own institutions. Effective production and distribution will be hard to establish and maintain.

In the interim, sacrifices of the general public will prompt nostalgic remembrances of the "good old days" of socialist rule—"at least we had bread at a controlled price".

Privatization sounds like a simple process to westerners who are used to a market oriented society. Former socialist economies planned factory investment to be highly specialized and interdependent. With the decline of the socialist system, there is no defined market structure to sell into. Even if new private owners of factories successfully convert their own operations, there are few supporting elements in the market **infrastructure**.

Failure to develop an adequate and functional market economy in a timely and effective manor will make former socialist states vulnerable to civil war and/or military dictatorship. Any such unfortunate turns will surely have ill effects on privatization and will actively challenge the globalization process.

Critical-Thinking Question:

1. Market economies have established distribution systems, both domestic and international. Discuss some important elements of such a system that are lacking in socialist or other command economies.

Notes

Notes